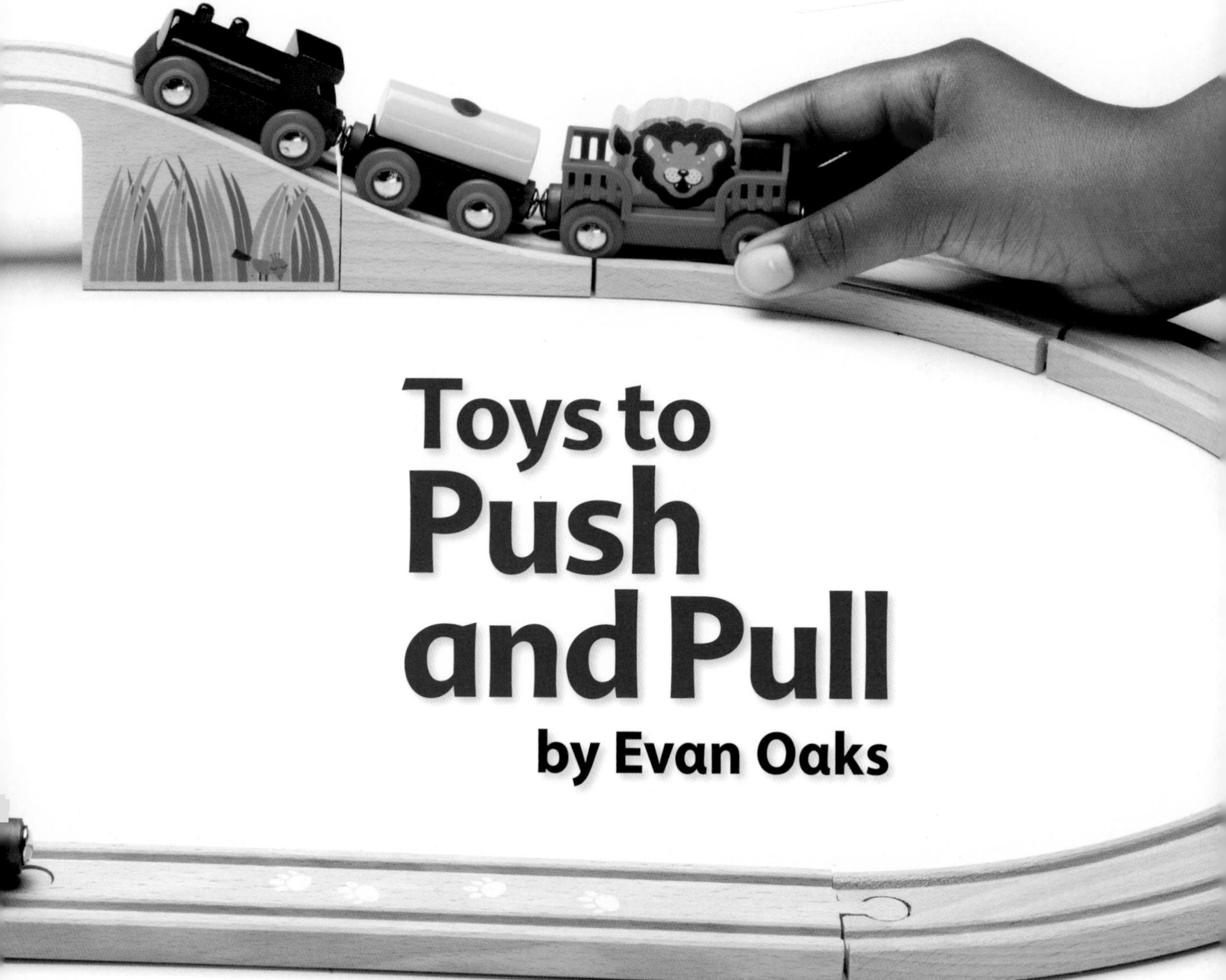

# Toys to Push and Pull

by Evan Oaks

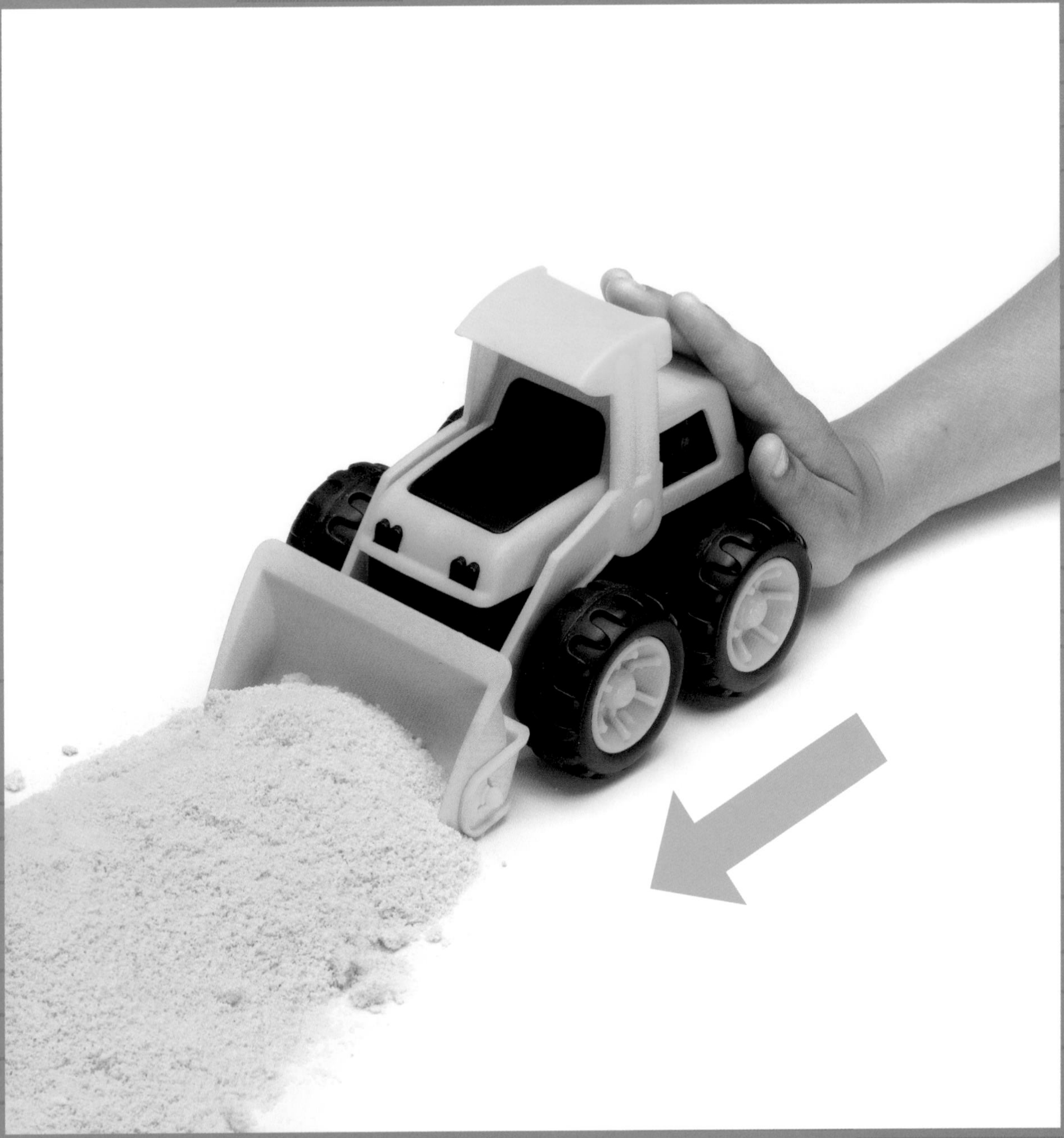

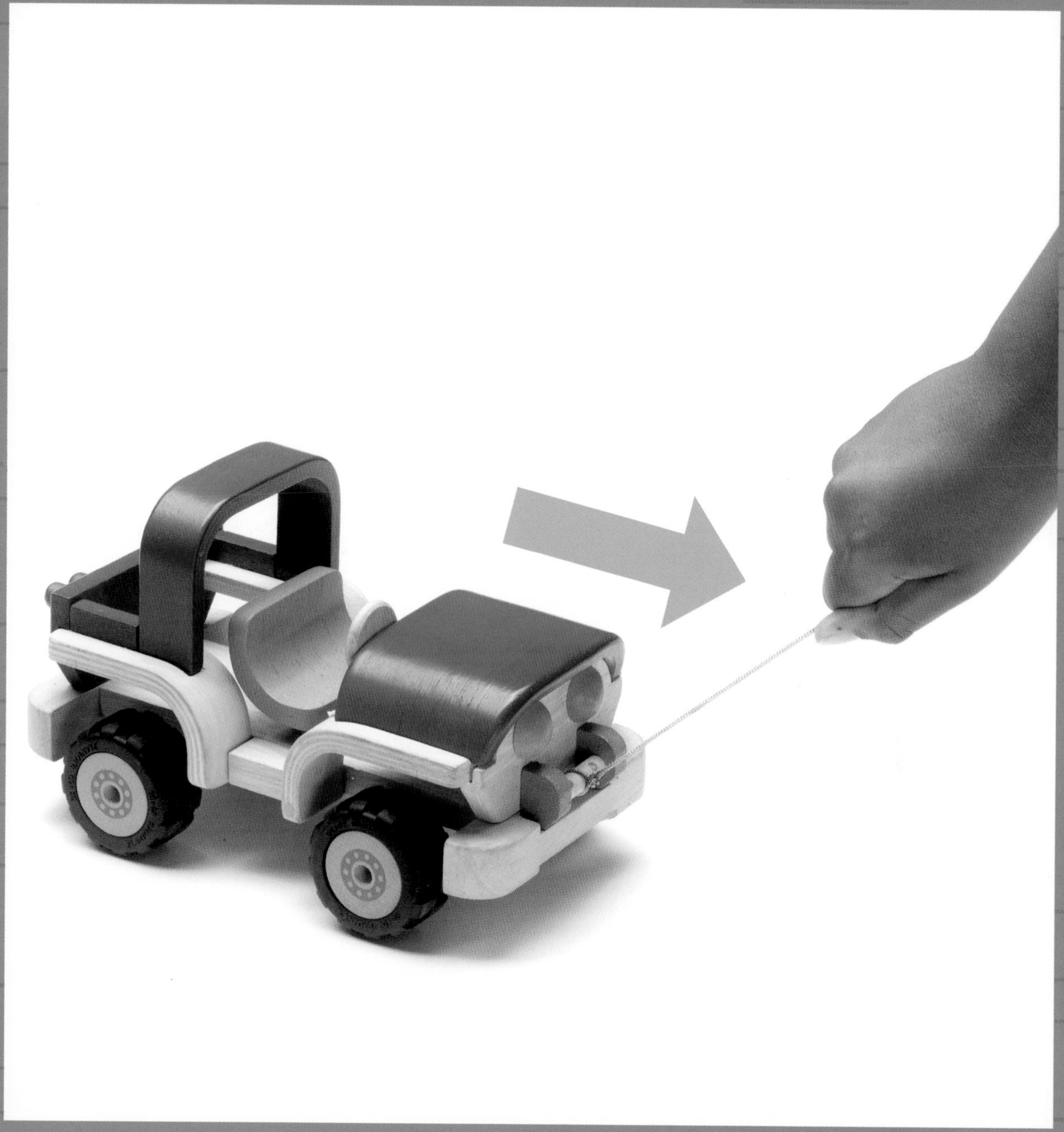

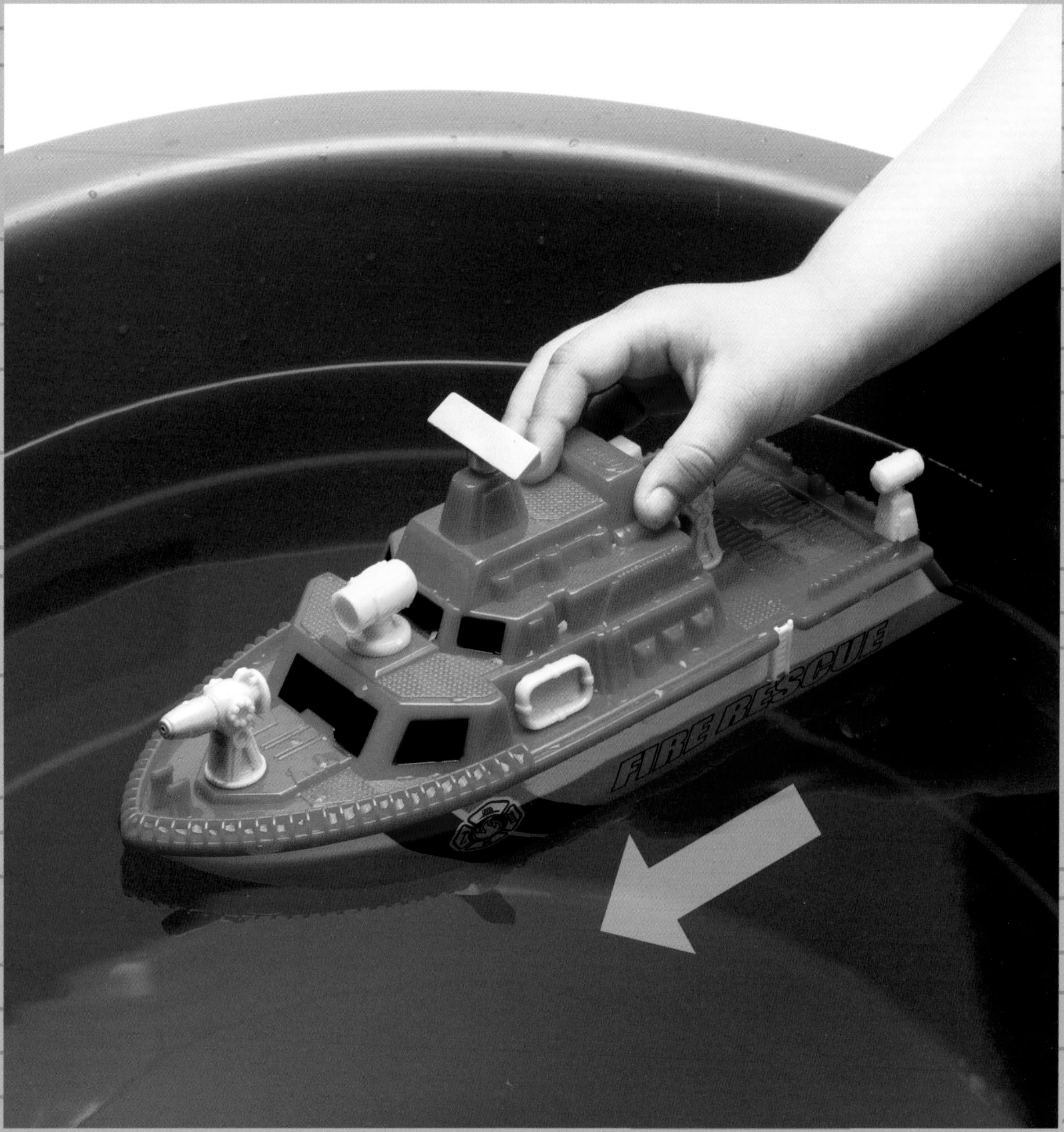
FIRE RESCUE

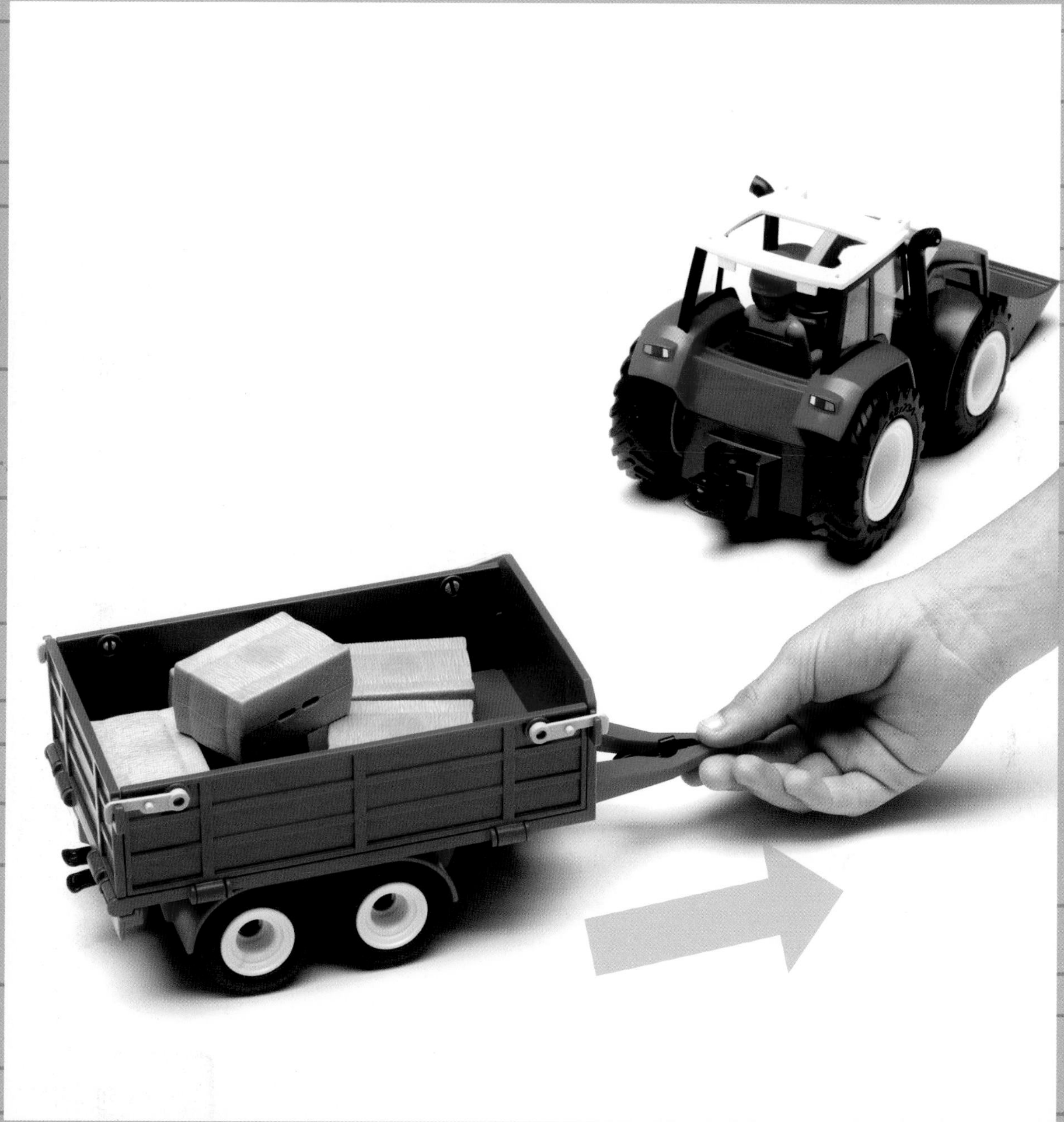

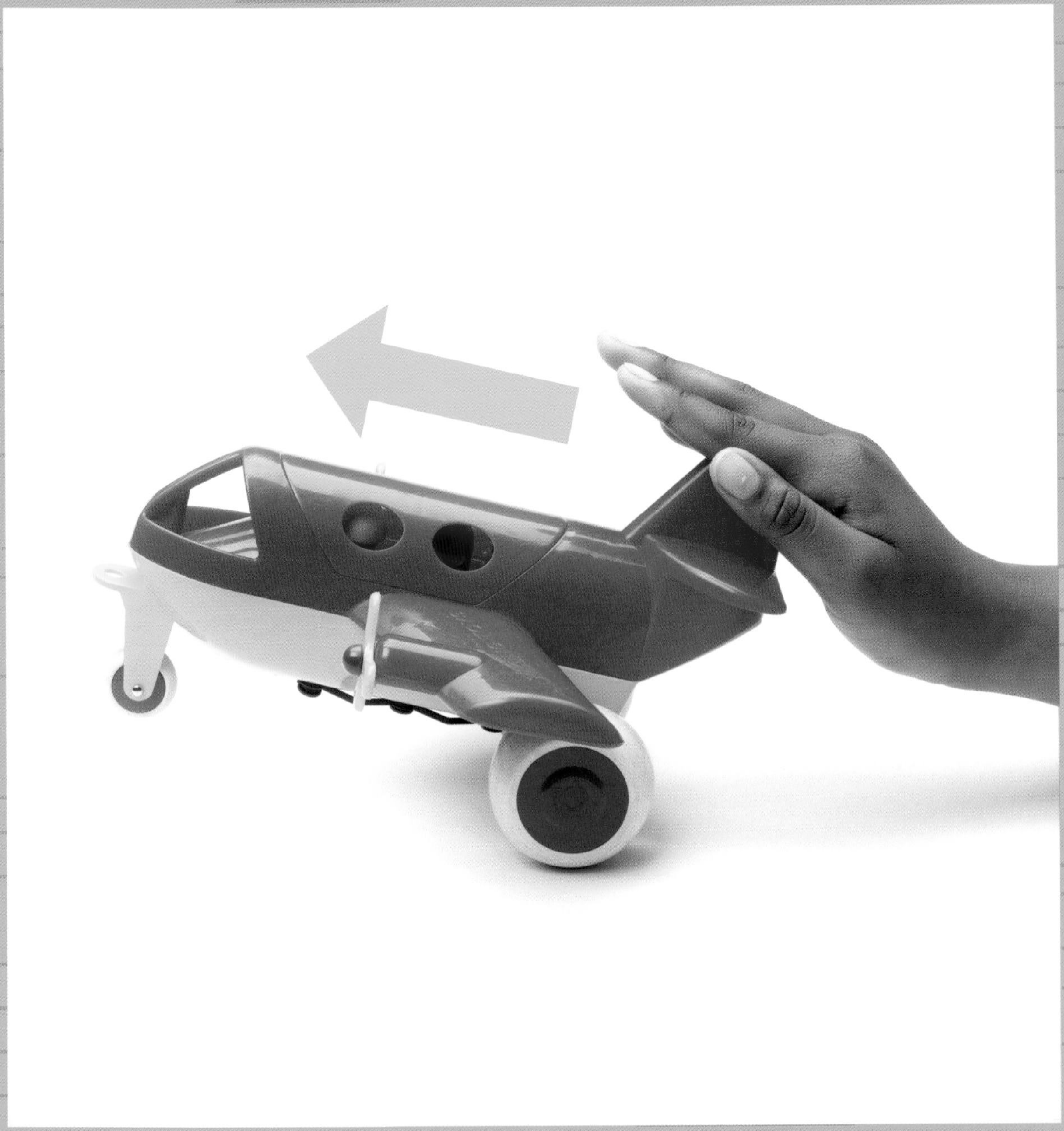

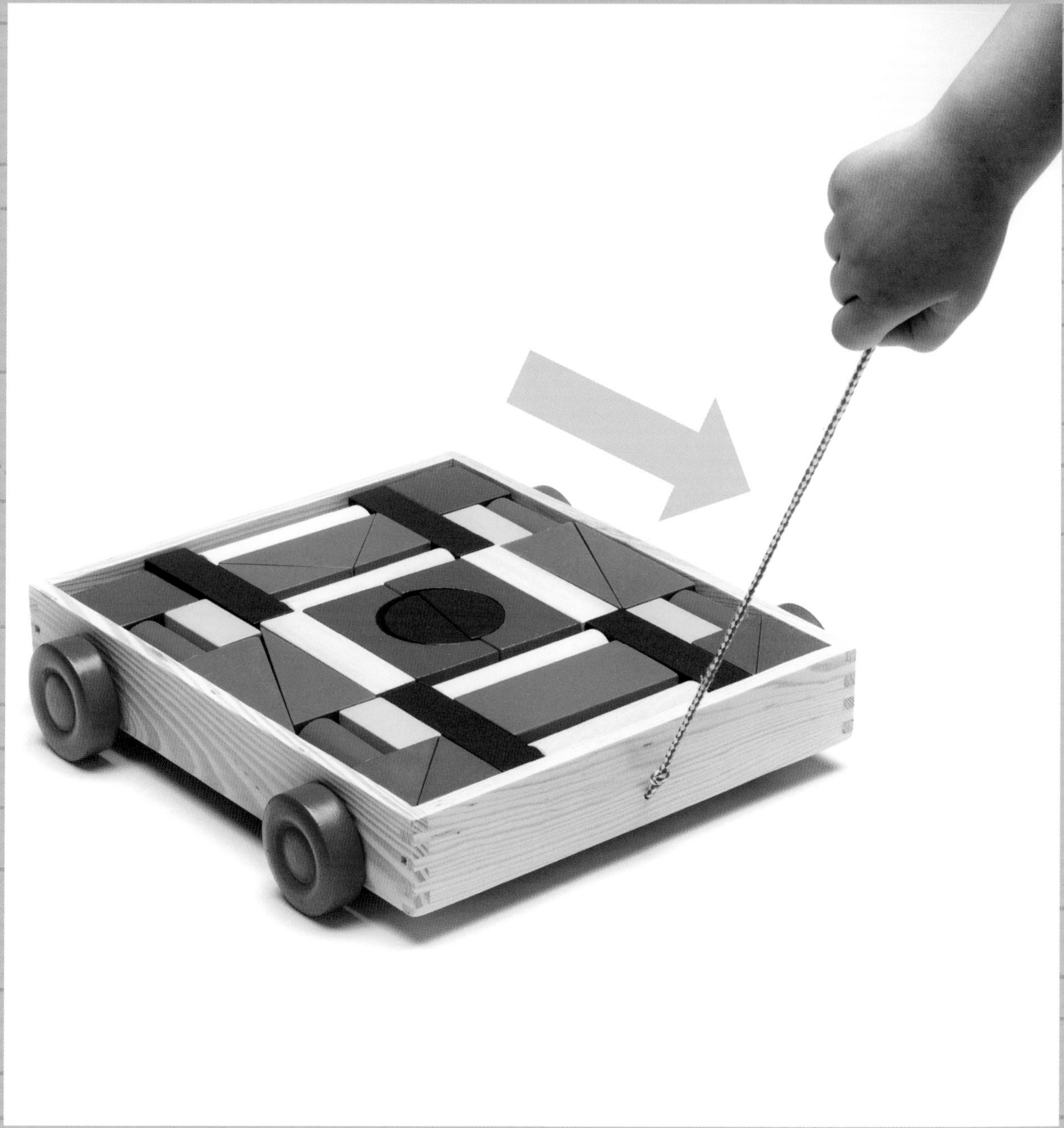

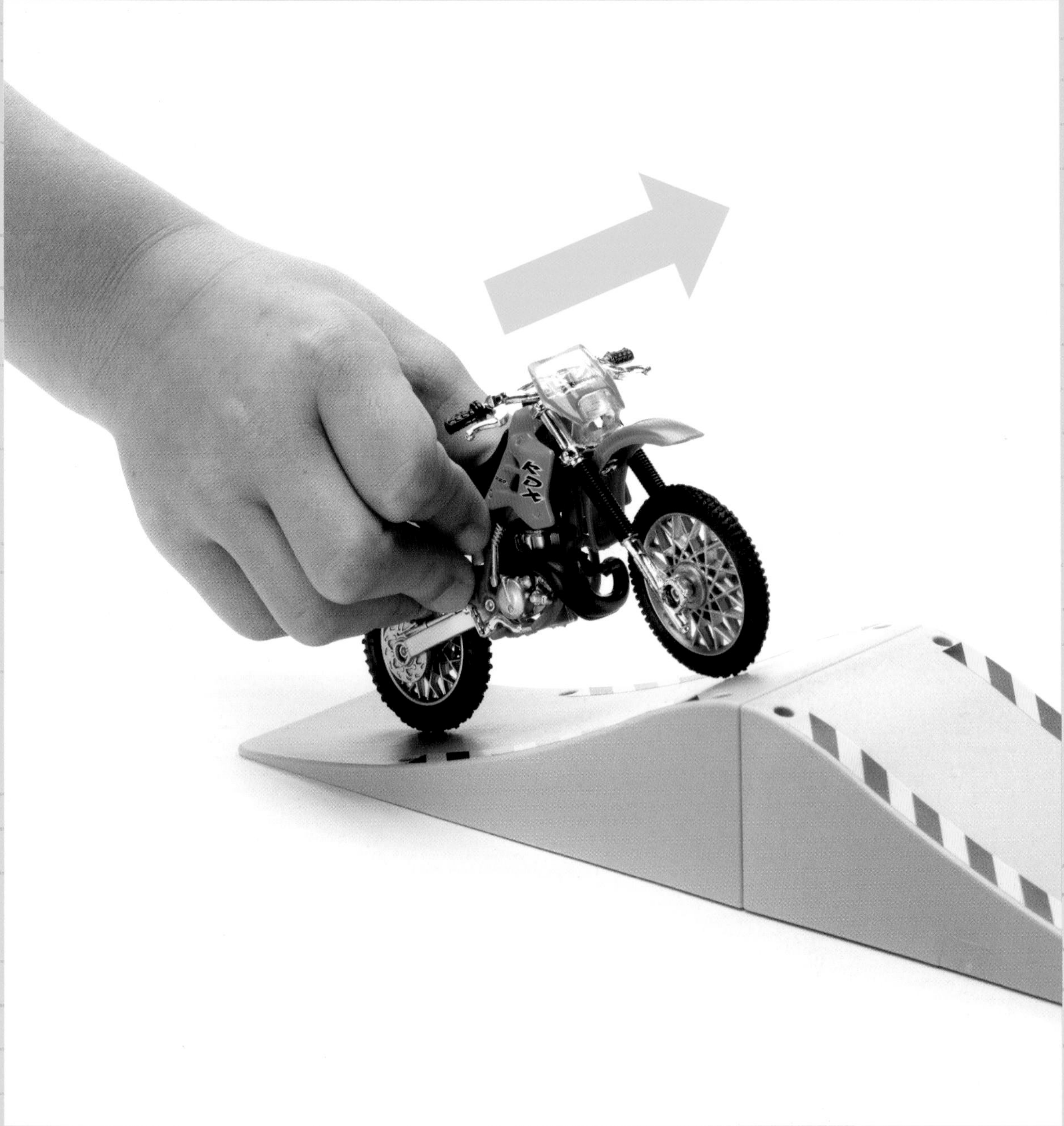